WICCA BOOK OF SHADOWS

Spells and Rituals for the Solitary Practitioner

Pierre Macedo

ISBN: 978-87-999829-4-3

First Edition 2021

Published by Leirbag Press, an imprint of Virgo Publishers.

contact@virgopublishers.com

Contents

INTRODUCTION

This book is a short version of The Ultimate Book of Magic and Witchcraft, and it is aimed at those who already know the basic concepts of magic and witchcraft. The following chapters present in the original book are not present in this one: general instructions, evocations, planetary magic, creating your own rituals and spells, and common questions and solutions.

The primary focus of this book is white magic, although it contains love and manipulation spells that can't be categorized other than black magic. The difference between these two terms is the intention of the practitioner. If you want to attract something into your life without directly causing harm to anyone, this is white magic. On the contrary, if you explicitly want to change the course of someone's life, this is black magic. Many, including myself, believe in something called karma that consists of reaping what you sow. If you do good things to others, that is what you will receive in this or the next life. It is up to you to decide which way you should go.

It is important to say, from the moment you start walking this path, you truly have to believe it, so that everything can work effectively. Your mind has the power of doing two essential things: to break magic spells and manifest your intentions. This applies in particular when we are working without the help of any spiritual beings. This type of spell is highly dependent on the magician or witch subconscious, while the ones cast with the help of some entity will depend more on the entity itself.

All the spells were carefully prepared, mixing ancient and modern magic. Although we don't need to do all the hard work our ancestors used to do, we can't completely get rid of some necessary steps, such as body and soul purification. These can dictate the success of our work because when doing magic, we are dealing with higher forces that don't share our human characteristics responsible for making us impure beings.

Now you have in your hands the key to change the course of your life. Use it wisely. I wish you good luck on your magical journey. May the universe conspire in your favor.

CHAPTER 1

BREAKING AND CLEANSING SPELLS

The first set of spells we are going to learn in this book are the ones you need to know before you start casting your owns. A magician or witch must know how to break any spell or to repel any negative energy because if you are targeting someone, you can also be targeted. When you enter into the occult world, it is like you are sending a message saying you are now part of that. It can be good because you attract to yourself the solutions for your problems that you could not see before, but it can be bad as well because you are also attracting forces that don't want to see you well. Let's look at how we can handle this.

Breaking Spells and Removing Negative Energies

This spell is a powerful one and is used to remove all the negativity from your life, including black magic. So, if you think that someone has cursed you or put a black magic spell on you, this is what you need. We will be working with the fire element and its ruler, the Archangel Michael.

Things You Will Need

- Two white candles.
- Incense (frankincense, orange, acacia, or calendula).
- Bible.

Step by Step

Purifying the place / Banishing with the fire element

I. Set up an altar in the south with the two candles and the incense. During this operation, you must always be facing south.

II. Hold one of the candles, light it, and say before the flame:

Hekas hekas este bebeloi.[1] *Far, far from this place, be the profane.*

III. Place your hand above the flame and say:

Creature of fire, I consecrate you and awaken you immediately. I purify this flame so that it can expand and remove all negativity, and bless everything it touches.

IV. Close your eyes and visualize the flame getting bigger and cleansing the space with the fire element. Then, quickly pass your hands through the flame to purify[2] yourself and say:

I invite all harmful forces to leave right now. By the creature of fire, may this place be blessed and I purified. May the salamanders burn those who try to come back. I now proclaim the sacred silence.

V. Stay in silence for a moment visualizing the place being cleansed.

Prayer to the Archangel Michael

I. Burn the incense.

II. Light the other candle. Vibrate[3] the name of Michael for a moment and concentrate on his energy. Say:

O Mighty and Powerful Archangel Michael, you who carries a flaming sword that fears all enemies, you who are a faithful protector of the Divine, you who reigns over the fiery flames of the fire element. I ask you to grant me the protection I need at this moment, so that all those who attempt some evil against me, may know the fury of him who is the Prince of the Archangels. If I am not worthy at this moment, make me worthy because I choose you as a guide on this journey of physical and spiritual strengthening. My mind is open to receive all the advice and teachings you have to offer me. May my aura be surrounded by your energy as a barrier that shields against all sorts of evil. The spiritual enemies, who now hear me, fear your power because they know they will suffer the consequences of trying to attack a protégé of yours. Hail Archangel Michael. Amen.

Invoking Michael

I. Say:

O Mighty and Powerful Archangel Michael, I invoke you. Michael, Prince of the Archangels, Prince of Virtues, Prince of Light, Guardian of Peace, Protector of the Divine, Ruler of Fire, I invoke you. I ask you, O Powerful Michael, to cleanse my energy field of all the influences that may be hindering and preventing the achievement of my goals. I ask you to break and cast away all kinds of witchcraft thrown at me. Before this flame of the fire element, I ask you to open all the paths that are closed in my life. So mote it be. Hail beloved Archangel Michael. Amen.

II. Recite the Psalm 85 to Michael; recite the Psalm 7 to finish the purification.

III. Thank the spirits:

I thank the fire elementals who participated in this purification. I thank you for your presence and your help, O Mighty Archangel Michael, and I say: see you soon.

IV. Stay in silence and put out the candles.

V. Let the incense burn to the end in a place without risk of fire

VI. You should lie down for 30 minutes after the ritual.

Space Cleansing

Easily cleanse your home or any place of negative energies.

Things You Will Need

- A glass of cold water with three teaspoons of salt.
- Incense (jasmine, poppy, myrtle, or sandalwood).

Step by Step

I. First, say:

Hekas hekas este bebeloi. Far, far from this place, be the profane.

II. Place your hand above the glass of water and say:

Creature of water, I consecrate you and awaken you immediately. I purify the essence of this fluid so that it can expel and remove all negativity, and bless everything it touches.

III. Sprinkle the space in which you are purifying with the consecrated water while saying:

I invite all harmful forces to leave right now. By the creature of water, may this place be blessed and I purified. I now proclaim the sacred silence.

IV. Stay in silence for a moment visualizing the place being cleansed. Concentrate on a violet flame cleansing and taking away all negative energy.

V. Burn the incense, and holding it, walk around the place while saying:

If there is any evil spirit here, leave now and go back to where you came from. I will not have mercy on you.

This is my place, and those who are not invited to be here will burn and disappear without a trace.

VI. Let the incense burn to the end in a place without risk of fire

Spell-Breaking Amulet

Amulets are objects commonly used for protection, but they can have other uses, such as luck, love, money, etc. In the last chapter, you have access to powerful ancient amulets that will prevent you from receiving any kind of evil energy. Our first objective with this tool is to create a custom amulet that will absorb all sorts of magic cast against you. If you suspect someone cursed or hexed you, this tool is right for you. Bear in mind what we are going to create is not only a simple inanimate object but a living entity that will work on the astral plane doing exactly what it was told at the time of its creation. You must destroy it as soon as its task is complete.

Things You Will Need

- A crystal, stone, pendant, coin, ring, etc. Choose one of these or another similar object.
- Salt.
- A glass of water.
- A white candle.
- Incense (any type).

Step by Step

Banishing

Let's cleanse the temple.

I. Burn an incense stick, and holding it, go to the east and say:

I invoke the guardians of the east to assist me in this rite. May the powers of the air cleanse this place of all negativity and evil spirits.

II. Walk around the place holding the incense and say:

I command all harmful and evil forces to leave right now.

By the powers of the air, I exorcise and purify this place.

III. Close your eyes and imagine the place being purified.

The ritual

I. Set up an altar in the center of the space in which you are working. Put the candle, salt, incense, water, and the object you chose over it.

II. Cast a circle wide enough for you and the altar.

III. Take some salt and throw it on the object while saying:

[Insert the name of the object], I exorcise you and purify you.

IV. Hold the object in your hand, take the incense, and go to the east. Say:

> *[Insert the name of the object], I awaken you now. By the powers of the air, you now live.*

Pass the object through the incense smoke.

V. Light the candle, take it, and go to the south. Say:

> *[Insert the name of the object], I awaken you now. By the powers of fire, you now live.*

Quickly pass the object through the flame.

VI. Take the water and go to the west. Say:

> *[Insert the name of the object], I awaken you now. By the powers of water, you now live.*

Sprinkle some water on the object.

VII. Take the salt and go to the north. Say:

> *[Insert the name of the object], I awaken you now. By the powers of the earth, you now live.*

Throw some salt on it.

VIII. Return to the center and hold the object with your two hands. Look at it and say:

> *[Insert the name of the object], you now live, and you are an amulet created to absorb all negative energy, black magic, and curse cast on me. Cleanse my body of all these unclean things. Then you must turn all this negativity into pure and harmless energy. Go now, and do your job.*

Keep the amulet for a maximum of 30 days.

Destroying the amulet

When you feel you are not under any spell anymore, you must destroy it. Important: even though you think it didn't work, you must destroy it. Don't be arrogant. You must say to the creature that its job is done.

I. Go to the same place where you created the amulet.

II. Perform the same banishing used to create it.

III. Set up the altar and cast a circle.

IV. Take some salt and throw it on the object while saying:

Creature of amulets, I exorcise you and purify you.

V. Take some more salt and go to the north. While looking at the object say:

Amulet, you completed your task; your work is done. I now revoke your creation. You don't exist anymore. By the powers of the earth, you don't live.

Again, throw some salt on it.

VI. Take the water and go to the west. Say:

Amulet, you completed your task; your work is done. I now revoke your creation. You don't exist anymore. By the powers of water, you don't live.

Sprinkle some water on the object.

VII. Light the candle, take it, and go to the south. Say:

Amulet, you completed your task; your work is done. I now revoke your creation. You don't exist anymore. By the powers of fire, you don't live.

Quickly pass the object through the flame.

VIII. Take the incense and go to the east. Say:

Amulet, you completed your task; your work is done. I now revoke your creation. You don't exist anymore. By the powers of the air, you don't live.

Pass it through the incense smoke.

IX. Close the circle and perform the Banishing Ritual of the Pentagram (see how in the next subject).

X. Throw the object in a river, sea, or bury it deep in the earth.

Ritual of the Pentagram

Created by the Hermetic Order of the Golden Dawn, this is a powerful ritual designed to banish any chaotic energy from your life and from the space in which you are working. It is widely used to open any magical ceremonies in order to banish all spirits that may be around and have the place cleansed to receive the forces we desire to work with. It can also protect you when it is practiced daily[4], strengthening your aura and making your energy field more balanced and stronger against any spirit with malicious intent or black magic spells.

Aleister Crowley, the most successful magician of the 20th century, writes in his notes on the Ritual of the Pentagram:

> *"Every man has a natural fortress within himself, the soul impregnable. Besides this central citadel, man also has an external fortress, the aura. It is the duty of every person to see that his aura is in good condition. There are two main methods for doing this. The first is by a performance two or three times daily of the Banishing Ritual of the Pentagram. Its main point is to establish in the astral four pentagrams, one in each quarter, and two hexagrams, one above, the other below, thus enclosing the magician, as it were, in a consecrated box. It also places in his aura the divine names invoked."*

Training Your Visualization

The downside of this ritual for beginners is its visualization process. You must visualize a lot of things, such as spheres of light, pentagrams, circles, crosses, etc. This is really important because all this is actually taking place on the astral plane. For example, if you are drawing a pentagram in the air, you must clearly visualize this pentagram in the air. You can do this with your eyes open or closed. I prefer to stay with my eyes closed because, at least for me, it eases the process. The visualization of colors is also a problem. The standard is to visualize the spheres in brilliant white light, and this can be easy or difficult for you. For me, I find white light a little bit hard to visualize. I prefer other colors like yellow or blue.

To develop your ability to visualize anything with your mind's eye, you need to practice it. Sit down or stand in a quiet place, close your eyes, and begin to imagine things around you, such as spheres of light and pentagrams. Draw anything you want in the air with your index finger and clearly visualize it. Try to keep your drawings active in your mind for as long as possible and don't lose focus. Another exercise you can do is to look at a picture for about three minutes, close your eyes, and try to reproduce it in your mind with all the details. Doing this on a daily basis, you will considerably improve your ability to see with your mind's eye.

Step by Step

The Qabalistic Cross

All the spheres of light in this ritual are formed from the same source of light. Other versions of it ask us to imagine those spheres without mentioning where their energy is coming from. I consider it a mistake, and that is why I created a modified version of the Qabalistic Cross.

I. Go to the east and face east. Stand with feet together and arms close to the body. Imagine that a sphere of brilliant white light is descending far from above your head. This sphere is about 10 inches or 25 centimeters in diameter, and now it is right just above your head.

II. With a dagger, wand, or your right index finger, touch the light and bring a fraction of it to the forehead. This smaller sphere is half the size of the one above your head. Touch the forehead and vibrate ATAH.

III. Touch the light again, but this time, point towards your feet and imagine the sphere of light descending to the ground. Vibrate MALKUTH.

IV. Now bring another sphere of light to the right shoulder. Touch the shoulder and vibrate VE-GEBURAH.

V. Bring another sphere to the left shoulder. Touch the shoulder and vibrate VE-GEDULAH.

VI. Put your hands together in front of your chest and vibrate LE-OLAHM. Now clearly imagine the four spheres of light forming a cross and this cross entering your body, filling it with pure light.

VII. Still with hands together vibrate AMEN.

Drawing the pentagrams

To trace the pentagrams in the air, you can use a dagger, a wand, or your index finger, preferably the right one. In this tutorial, we are going to work with the index finger.

I. In the east, facing east, draw in the air the Banishing Pentagram of Earth and then bring the point of your finger to its center. Vibrate[5] the name YHVH.

Figure 1. The Banishing Pentagram of Earth

The arrow indicates the direction you must draw the pentagram.

II. Without moving your finger in any other direction, start tracing a circle while you move to the south. In the south, trace the Banishing Pentagram of Earth again. Bring your finger to the center and vibrate ADNI.

III. Continue the semi-circle to the west and again trace the pentagram bringing your finger to its center. Vibrate AHIH.

IV. Repeat the same process in the north. Vibrate the name AGLA ATAH GIBOR LE-OLAHM.

V. Now complete the circle bringing your finger again to the center of the pentagram you drew in the east.

VI. Now in the east, stay in cross position (feet together and arms extended) and say:

Before me, the great Archangel RAPHAEL (vibrate).

Behind me, the great Archangel GABRIEL (vibrate).

At my right hand, the great Archangel MICHAEL (vibrate).

At my left hand, the great Archangel AURIEL (vibrate).

VII. Now say:

About me, flame the pentagrams.

Imagine the circle and the pentagrams in white flames.

And in the column shines the six-rayed star.

Imagine two hexagrams, one under and one above you, shining and forming a grid of light around your body.

VIII. Repeat the Qabalistic Cross, and it is done.

Pronunciation Guide

Learn how to pronounce the words and names used in this ritual as they are pronounced in Hebrew.

Table 1. Pronunciation guide

ATAH (You are)	ah-tah
MALKUTH (the Kingdom)	mah-hoot
VE-GEBURAH (and Power)	veh-geh-boo-rah[6]
VE-GEDULAH (and Glory)	veh-geh-doo-lah
LE-OLAHM (forever)	leh-olahm
YHVH	ye-hoh-vah
ADNI	ah-doh-nye
AHIH	eh-heh-yeh
AGLA	ah-gah-lah
GIBOR	gee-bor[7]
RAPHAEL	rah-fah-el
GABRIEL	gah-vree-el
MICHAEL	mee-hah-el
AURIEL	au-hee-el

The above pronunciations and the ones found in the Appendix of this book were transcribed after listening many times to audios of native Hebrew speakers. I did the best I could, but unfortunately, English has some limitations when we try to transcribe sounds from other languages.

Endnotes

1. This is a phrase taken from the ancient Eleusinian Mysteries that means "far, far from this place, be the profane."
2. If you don't know how to pass your hands through the flame of a candle without getting burn, please don't do this.
3. This means pronouncing a word aloud, vibrating the syllables.
4. In order to practice the Banishing Ritual of the Pentagram on a daily basis, you also need to practice the Invoking Ritual of the Pentagram (see the Appendix). Otherwise, your energy will be unbalanced.
5. All the four names of God in this ritual must be intensely vibrated to the limits of the universe.
6. The "e" in "veh" and "geh" sounds pretty similar to the one in "eight." And the "g" in "geh" sounds like the one in "guide."
7. The "g" in "gee" sounds like the one in "guide."

CHAPTER 2

LOVE SPELLS

There is a big chance you are reading this book mainly because of this chapter. You may be hungry to know how to cast some spells to bring back the love of your life, and I promise you will know it, but first, I must say there is no such thing as a love spell. Love is the most beautiful feeling a human can have, and it happens naturally. Love spells are about forcing someone to like you and changing someone's life. This is not love but persuasion and manipulation. And this is why love spells belong to the category of black magic. When you change someone's life for your benefit or the benefit of others without his or her consent, you are doing black magic. You may be thinking, what is the problem? Well, if you believe in karma, there is a big problem: you are bringing bad karma to you because we can't mess with someone's life without paying for that. In case you don't care about it, you are good to go. Decide for yourself if you should or should not cast this kind of spell.

Love Spell 01

This spell will make the person you love think about you all the time.

Things You Will Need

- An apple.
- A rose flower.
- A red paper heart with the name, date of birth, and zodiac sign of the beloved person written on it.
- A red paper heart with your name, date of birth, and zodiac sign written on it.
- Seven wooden toothpicks.
- A glass of water with three teaspoons of salt.
- A clean knife.

Step by Step

Banishing

I. Place your hand above the glass of water and say:

Creature of water, I consecrate you and awaken you immediately. I purify the essence of this fluid so that it can expel and remove all negativity, and bless everything it touches.

II. Sprinkle the space in which you are purifying with the consecrated water while saying:

I invite all harmful forces to leave right now. By the creature of water, may this place be blessed and I purified. I now proclaim the sacred silence.

III. Stay in silence for a moment visualizing the place being cleansed. Concentrate on a violet flame cleansing and taking away all negative energy.

IV. When you feel ready and purified, start the ceremony.

The ritual

I. Sprinkle some of the holy water on the paper heart with the name of the beloved person written on it. Hold the paper and focus entirely on the person in question and say:

> *Creature of paper, I consecrate you, so that you represent [insert the name of the person]. You are [insert the name of the person] in body, soul, and spirit. You are the head and mind of [insert the name of the person]. You are a connection with [insert the name of the person], and you are the key to the heart of [insert the name of the person], born on [insert the date of birth of the person].*

II. Stay focused until you feel you have created a connection with your target.

III. When you feel the connection was created, hold the apple and say:

> *Fruit of lust, fruit of passion, fruit of seduction, and temptation, now send your powers and your energy to my rite.*

IV. Concentrate on passion and lust, thinking about the person and bringing this feeling into you.

V. Hold the rose flower and say:

> *Mystical flower of the holy mysteries, flower of love and power. Remember now the ancestral knowledge and send your sensuality and your love. Rose, I invoke your love mysteries.*

VI. Think about what you want and begin to visualize your desire, repeating it until you are tired and feeling a powerful energy in you. This takes from 10 to 20 minutes.

VII. Take the paper heart with your name written on it, sprinkle some water, and say:

Creature of paper, I consecrate you, so that you represent me, I [insert your name] in body, soul, and spirit. You are my head and my mind, you are a connection with me, and so receive my energy.

VIII. Put a drop of saliva on this same paper. Ideally, you should put a drop of blood, but saliva will work as well.

IX. Then, using a clean knife, cut the apple in half vertically and remove the seeds which will be used at the end of this ritual. Place the paper with the name of the person you love on one part of the apple and the paper with your name over it so that the names are facing each other.

X. Rejoin the two halves of the apple and start sticking the toothpicks while saying:

May love, friendship, and fellowship flourish between the heart of [insert the name of the person] and my heart. So that together, I [insert your name] and [insert the name of the person] can share the purest love, the love that keeps the flame of life alive, powerful love, glorious, heavenly, and dreamy.

XI. With the last toothpick, stick the rose flower on the top of the apple. Raise the apple and raise the energy, thinking about your goal.

XII. Keep the apple seeds in a little bag for as long as you think is necessary.

XIII. Dispose of the apple in the woods or somewhere else surrounded by trees.

Love Spell 02: Working with Lilith

Everything About Lilith

Most of the things one can find about Lilith on the internet or other magic books are incomplete or wrong. Some describe her as Adam's first wife, a demon, a sex goddess, etc. No one seems to agree on what she really is, and, to be frank, we don't need to, as I am going to show in the next paragraph. The descriptions of her powers and what she can do for those who ask her for help are also limited, considering she is a spirit with so much potential but unknown to most of the occultists. So, before proceeding to the actual work, I am going to show what Lilith is and what you can get from her.

Lilith, Laylah, Darkat, Layil is the embodiment of the night. She has black hair, red eyes, and the animals that represent her are the snake, the dog, and the bull. She likes apple, peach, white lilies, red roses, red wine, pure water, attar of roses. She is the angel of prostitution of Zoroastrian Kabbalah, being the mother of seduction, illusion, abortion, freedom, and prostitutes. She is a sorceress and works hard on sexual matters, passions, dreams, and vampirism. For paganism, she is a moon goddess, and in orthodox Judaism, she is a part of Shekinah (feminine presence or manifestation of the Jewish God). In modernity, she went through many changes and became the feminine side of Satan. She is everything that came before the Jewish God and everything that opposes him; that is, she is good and bad at the same time. She can do anything, but her specialty is witchcraft and sexuality. For her, always white or red candles. She is the mistress of dreams, and through dreams and sex, she sucks the vital energy of people, which is the energy present in semen or blood, the energy of one's life. There is no need to classify her as a god, angel, or demon because she is an ancient and powerful spirit, and that is enough for us to show her all due respect.

She, like all the other spirits, has two sides that one may define as evil and good, which I don't agree with. The definition of what is evil and what is good is so human and simplistic that it can't be completely applied to the astral plane. The evil side of Lilith is mainly credited to her mother of abortion personality and because sometimes she may not like being evoked, and so she may be a little rude, especially if you have nothing that interests her. But since we are not going to actually evoke Lilith in our spell and we are not going to ask her anything related to babies or kids, everything should run smoothly in our operation.

Things You Will Need

- A saucer.
- A red or white candle.
- Two strawberries or apples.
- A red paper or plush heart with the name of the beloved person written behind it.
- The seal of Lilith.
- Sterilized needle (optional).

Step by Step

Banishing

Say:

In the name of Layil, mistress of the night, of wrath and storms, I command all negativity to leave this place. By the power of Layil, mistress of destruction and punishment, I send back everything thrown at me, and I break the obstacles that prevent my magic.

PROCUL, O PROCUL ESTE PROFANI. Profane and unclean spirits go away.

The ritual

I. Arrangements

Everything used in this spell you put on the saucer. The strawberries or apples are used to decorate it. Arrange everything in a way that pleases you. Put the seal of Lilith in front of the saucer.

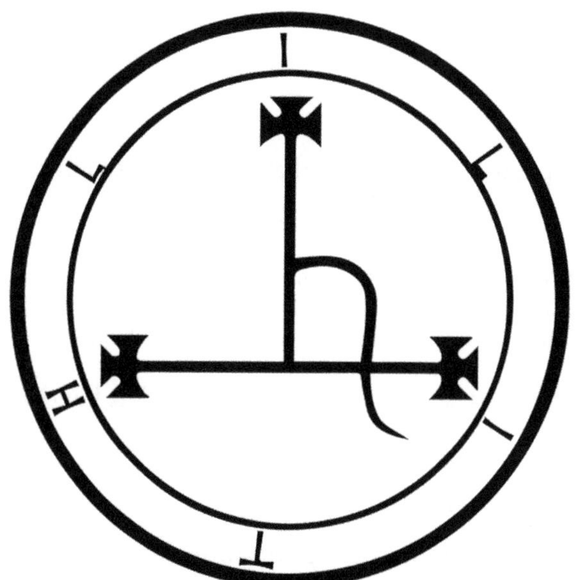

Figure 2. The seal of Lilith

II. Invocation

Lilith, holy angel of prostitution, hear me.

I invoke you, mother of rebellion and seduction.

Look at me now with your red eyes.

Ignite me with the fire of desires and with your lust.

Drown me in the lakes of passion.

Put in my hands the apple of desire, the pear of sweetness, and the peach of lust.

Now build the carpet of lilies for my walk.

Put in my body the aroma of the rose, the burning of the pepper, and in my lips the honey.

Open the doors of your world to me; bring me joy and achievements.

Give me the treasures of this land and let me be the temptation.

Hail Laylah.

The sacred act of masturbation

First, I need to point out that masturbation, when used in rituals, is considered a holy act. Bear in mind that you are not masturbating to have fun but to release the necessary energy for the spell to work.

III. Focus on Lilith for a few minutes and vibrate her name.

IV. Begin the sacred act (masturbation) with the left hand visualizing your desire and keeping in mind that it is coming true. Hold your orgasm as long as you can, and when you cannot, ejaculate and put in your mouth the elixir of life (semen). Spit it on the candle and spread it, "masturbate" the candle while strongly visualizing your desires, and when you feel a force inside of you wanting to leave, you light the candle, as if it had ejaculated and was sending the energy to your goal.

V. Say:

In the name of Lilith, the spell begins.

By the power of Lilith, [insert the name of the person] is mine.

I now change your mind.

Just as my heart is yours, so is my desire.

You love me; you are attracted to me. In me, is your passion and your heart.

VI. Pierce your finger and drip three drops of blood on the heart. (optional)

VII. Then hold the heart and think as if you were the person you love:

I love [insert your name].

I want you, I desire you, I need you.

You are the reason I wake up every day.

Our love is greater than ourselves.

Our love is what makes us one.

My heart I give to you, and forever, we shall be together.

VIII. Let the candle burn to the end in a place without risk of fire. Keep the heart with you or bury it, preferably in the woods.

Note: this spell is ideal for men because of the masturbation part. If you are a woman, you can also perform the sacred act of masturbation, but you will not be able to use the elixir of life that only men possess. You can use a drop of blood to replace the semen and give energy to the spell. It will work in the same way.

Love Spell 03: Working with Baal

Everything About Baal

Baal is an ancient god who was worshiped by the Canaanites and Phoenicians. His name means Lord. In the Goetia, he is considered a powerful king who governs in the east and has legions of spirits under his command. Baal Hadad is the god of storm, rain, fertility, abundance, and ruler of the world. To work with him, one must offer him water representing harmony, balance, and destruction; salt representing plenty or death; fruits, grains, and wine. To get in touch with Baal, it is necessary to have a representation of him that can be a physical or mental image, in addition to a prayer. You must be patient when working with this god, and worshiping him with daily prayers and offerings is the best way to get his attention. Baal is such a versatile god that this same spell can be used for other purposes.

Things You Will Need

- A glass of water.
- Fruits and grains.

Step by Step

Purification

I. Raise the glass of water and say:

In the name of Baal Hadad, Lord of Order and Rain, I consecrate the essence of this fluid to purify everything it touches.

II. Sprinkle the space with the water and drink some of it.

The ritual

I. Opening

I come forth to perform this sacred act. It is my wish to connect with Baal and with the holy Elohim. I greet the gods of the past; I salute the gods of Canaan, the land of prosperity and happiness.

Hail El, the father of mankind. Hail El Elyon. Abu, Abu Adami; Abu, Abu Shanima (in the Canaanite language, it means Father, Father of Man; Father, Father of Time).

II. Think of Baal, in his aspects, focus on him, and invoke:

I invoke the sacred name of Baal Shamem, the Lord of Heaven and Thunder.

Baal son of El, Baal Aliyan, the one who prevails.

Baal Lord of Justice and Grains, Baal Son of Dagon, Baal Zephon, Lord of the North, Baal Anthar, Baal Brathy, Baal Karmelos, Baal Marqo, Baal Gad, Baal Hammom, and all the other names that you may want to be called, I invoke you.

Baal Reginon, Lord of Raven and Thunder, Lord of Destruction, come to me.

Baal Hadad, Lord of Rain and Fertility.

Hail Baal, who defeats Mot and Yam.

III. Offer fruits and grains to Baal.

IV. Prayer

Baal, Mighty and Powerful God, I come before you to humbly ask for your help.

I am in love with someone who is not in love with me, and I wish to change that.

May your powers make [insert the name of the person you love] loves me the way I love him (her).

May your powers make [insert the name of the person you love] desires me the way I desire him (her).

Because I know Lord Baal, from now on, he (she) can't live without me.

His (her) mind is now changed, and there is love between us.

Hail Baal Hadad. Amen.

V. Meditation

Baal, Mighty Lord, you who have turned away from humanity because of blasphemy, come to me. I call you with a holy and reverent mind.

VI. Silence your mind and your thoughts, focusing on Baal. Keep silent as if you were waiting for something.

Love Spell 04: Working with Aphrodite

This spell is not to bring someone you love, it will bring someone that will love you into your life, and this is completely different from the other love spells we learned so far. Here we have a case of white magic because you will not mess with anyone's life but will just ask for your true love to come into your life. So, we can conclude there is no karma involved here, in case you believe it.

Brief Note on Aphrodite

Aphrodite is a goddess of Greek mythology, also worshiped by the Romans. She is the daughter of Zeus and Dione, and her Roman equivalent is the Goddess Venus. She is the goddess of beauty, fertility, love, and sexuality.

Things You Will Need

- An apple.
- Seven strawberries.
- Seven red rose petals.
- Seven cloves.

- Honey.
- A red candle.
- A white candle.
- A white bowl.
- A glass of water.

This ritual should take place on Friday, the day of Venus.

Step by Step

Purification

I. First, you need to purify yourself physically and spiritually. Take a bath to cleanse your body, and wear clean clothes. Meditate and clear your mind of all unholy thoughts. If it is possible for you and if you want to, you can go without eating meat for 24 hours before the ritual.

II. Start the purification by saying the Homeric Hymn 23 to the Son of Cronus:

I will sing of Zeus, chiefest among the gods and greatest, all-seeing, the lord of all, the fulfiller who whispers words of wisdom to Themis as she sits leaning towards him. Be gracious, all-seeing Son of Cronos, most excellent and great.

III. Then say:

Hekas hekas este bebeloi. Far, far from this place, be the profane.

IV. Place your hand above the glass of water and say:

Creature of water, in the name of Zeus, Son of Cronus, I purify you.

V. Sprinkle the space in which you are purifying with the consecrated water while saying:

O theoi genoisthe apotropoi kakon. May the gods turn away evils.

The ritual

I. Light the white candle and say the Homeric Hymn 10 to Aphrodite:

Of Cythera, born in Cyprus, I will sing. She gives kindly gifts to men; smiles are ever on her lovely face, and lovely is the brightness that plays over it. Hail, goddess, queen of well-built Salamis and sea-girt Cyprus; grant me a cheerful song. And now I will remember you and another song also.

II. Proceed to the invocation:

Aphrodite, goddess of love, I invoke you.

Daughter of Zeus, goddess of pleasure, goddess of beauty, goddess of sexuality, I invoke you.

I beg for your help with the mysteries of love and sex.

Throw your ancient mysteries at me.

Open the gates of love and pleasure in my life.

Bring me love and make me beautiful and attractive.

No man (woman) will look at me without desire, but among them, a special one will come to me.

He (she) is the one who loves me.

Hail Aphrodite, goddess of many virtues.

III. Put the rose petals and the cloves in the bowl, and say:

In the name of Aphrodite, I will be beautiful and attractive.

IV. Put the strawberries and apple, and say:

In the name of Aphrodite, I will have pleasure in my life.

V. Cover everything with honey and say:

In the name of Aphrodite, love will come into my life.

VI. Light the red candle and say:

So mote it be.

VII. Bury the contents of the bowl in the woods or somewhere else surrounded by trees.

CHAPTER 3

BEAUTY SPELLS

This type of spell I could easily have included in the previous chapter since your problems with love may be only a matter of lack of confidence in yourself, and the proper gods can help you to achieve that and even the beauty pattern you think you don't have. But maybe your problems are not related to love, and you just want to feel beautiful, to change the person you think you are, to look at the mirror and see something that pleases you, and to be praised by others for your physical characteristics. So, if this is your case, the spells in this chapter will certainly help you with that.

Beauty spells work, both changing your perception of yourself and your body shape as well. The first effect of these spells is to make the person who cast it to accept the fact that they are beautiful indeed. When you change your perception of yourself, people will also start looking at you in a different way. The other effect you can expect are physical changes in your body, and this can happen in many scales from soft to a complete disappearance of the unwanted characteristic. What one must bear in mind is that depending on the problem, significant changes can't occur physically. Supposing a small person wants to grow little inches more, but they are not in the growth stage anymore, the desired effect is unlikely to happen. The same goes for someone with a big nose where little differences can be noticed, but it will not have a considerable reduction. On the other hand, other problems like spots, scars, wrinkles, hair, etc., can be completely resolved.

Frey and Freya

Frey is a Norse god, King of the Vanir, god of prosperity, harvest, mysteries, virility, and fertility. Frey is Freya's brother, goddess of beauty, love, sensuality, magic, and protective goddess of pregnant women. Frey and Freya bring together all the characteristics that the word beauty carries. They are powerful gods always willing to help those who invoke them because, like most gods, they have been forgotten by mankind.

Figure 3. Frey

Figure 4. Freya

Things You Will Need

- A red or white candle.
- A glass of water, wine, or mead.
- A little plate.
- An image of Freya (you can use the Figure 4 of this book or search on Google for one that pleases you better).
- Some seeds or grains.

Step by Step

Pre-ritual

I. Take a bath to purify your body.

II. Say out loud:

Bearer of the mighty hammer Mjölnir.

Hail Thor Veu.

III. Go to the north, make the hammer sign, and say:

Hammer of Thor, protects us in the northern paths. All suffering must go away.

The hammer sign:

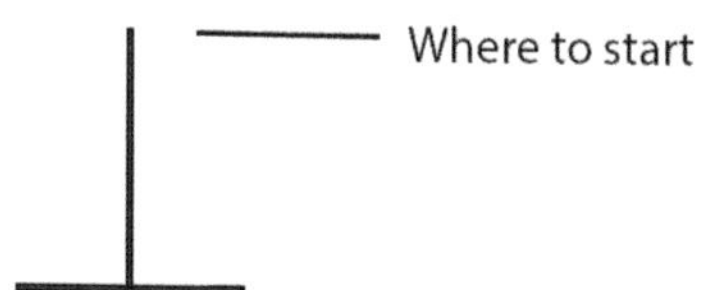

Figure 5. The hammer sign

IV. Go to the east, make the hammer sign, and say:

Hammer of Thor, protects us in the eastern paths. All suffering must go away.

V. Repeat the same process in the south and west.

VI. Return to the north, looking at the sky, make the hammer sign, and say:

Hammer of Thor, give us the blessing of the heavens.

VII. Looking at the ground, make the hammer sign, and say:

Hammer of Thor, give us the blessing of the womb of the Earth.

VIII. Stay in the Algiz position.

Algiz position: stand with your arms extended above your head, forming a 90-degree angle between them. Feel that your body is like a tree, visualizing the trunk and the crown, and feeling the force flowing through you, revering the sacredness of your body while vibrating the name ALGIZ.

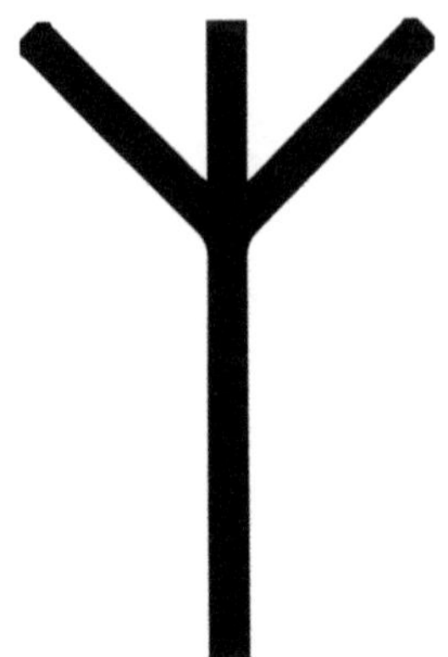

Figure 6. The Algiz position

Algiz is one of the most powerful runes; it illustrates a horned animal, a tree, and a man with the arms stretched out. Algiz describes the search and contact with the higher powers, and how to receive their protection. The Algiz rune can be seen as the awakening of sexual forces and how they can activate the warrior spirit. In divination, this rune can be interpreted as the awakening of inner forces and the effort to attain divinity.

The ritual

I. Place your hands above the altar and say:

> *I bless and make this altar a sacred place for the service of Freya, banishing all profane and impure influences. May my mind, in this blessed place, also be blessed. As Heimdall guards the Bifrost bridge, may this place be guarded against all forces that oppose my rite today.*

II. Meditate with Freya for some minutes. Stay in the Algiz position and invoke:

> *Frú Freya (frú = frau = lady), goddess of pleasures and sensuality, goddess of love and fertility, wealth, and earthly pleasures. We know you, mistress of life, in the*

field in fertile beasts, but also in the wombs of women. Goddess of pleasures and affection, I greet you for the many delights in Midgard. I thank you for life, for fertility, and when the dead warriors fall on battlefields, you gather the heroes and take them to your hall of pleasures. Come, Freya, in the form of a cat.

Falcon feathers woman, lady of the Seidr. I invoke you lady who cries tears of gold; witch, warrior, bearer of the Brisingamen.

Hail Freya.

III. Focus on Freya for one minute and say:

Goddess of love and lust, welcome.

Daughter of Niord, welcome.

Sister of Lord Frey, welcome.

Goddess of the Vanir, welcome.

Wife of Od, welcome.

Lady of magic, welcome.

Lady of the Valkyries, welcome.

Lady of desire, welcome.

Lady of wealth, welcome.

Lady of beauty, be welcome.

IV. Relax your body and mind focusing on the image of Freya. Take a deep breath and relax more and more, mentally calling for Freya until you feel a force moving your consciousness. Then say:

Come to me, Vanadis, to receive this sacrifice prepared for you. Do not take your gifts from me, but continue to send them into my life, in the prosperity and rejoicing of sensuality in all things. May through this sincere and simple ceremony, I can dry the golden tears of your face. Most beautiful goddess, I invoke you.

V. Raise the glass of water and say:

And I offer you a sacrifice. Not in blood, but the grace of my human efforts, my struggle, and my devotion. May the covenant between man and gods be strong in our fight to defend Asgard or against those who wish to enslave the friends of the gods in Midgard.

VI. Pour a little of the liquid into the dish and say:

Freya, accept this gift, not from a slave or a servant because I have no master. Not as a form of appeasement because everything is fine between us, but as a sign of our communion and likeness.

Show Freya the other offerings at the altar. If it is a liquid, pour it into the same dish. Light the candle offering its flame to Freya and say:

Freya, you received my sacrifice, symbolized by the offerings. Now send your blessings and powers to me so that I can grow and fulfill my desires now. Share your gifts with me.

Hail Freya.

VII. Invoking Frey

King of the Vanir.

Frey, god of the grains.

Warrior without weapon who gave your sword for love.

Yngvi, you make the grains flow in the spring.

God of male beauty, virility, and splendor.

Lord of the light elves.

Lord of happiness and fertility.

I salute you, son of Niord, Freya's brother.

VIII. Put some of the seeds or grains on the plate, and pour a little more of the liquid saying:

Lord Frey, accept my sacrifice.

IX. Relax, focus on Frey and Freya, and say:

Hail, Hail to the mystery.

Frey, Freya, gods of mysteries.

King and Queen of the Vanir.

Gods of beauty, gods of wealth.

Goddess of love and passion.

Goddess of sensuality, magic, battle, and seduction.

God of the fertile fields, beauty, and virility.

God of splendor, happiness, and fertility.

Now grant the necessary power to my magic.

Bring me the visions, awaken the intuition, and show me what I cannot see.

If I dream about verses, bring me the songs, lend me your power.

I now desire to obtain sensuality and beauty, the gifts of your nature.

X. Begin to visualize the type of beauty you want to have, the imperfections of the skin fading, the shape of the face, body. Imagine a red energy filling your body and shaping you. This energy brings you a sweet and feminine beauty, a feminine sensuality, a masculine beauty and virility at the same time. Also, visualize this aura attracting passion, friendships, affection, powers to seduce, to enchant. When you feel this intense energy inside you, describe with your words what that beauty is for you.

XI. Visualize Freya and Frey, giving you the powers of sensuality, beauty, love, fertility.

Lofna, in the name of Frey and Freya, send your blessings: betrayal, passion, and homosexuality.

Gersemi and Hnoss, in the name of Frey and Freya, send your blessings: love, beauty, and maternity.

XII. Visualize the desired aspects again, but this time more strongly and fixed on you, as if they went from your interior to your exterior.

XIII. Take a deep breath pulling the energy of Frey and Freya into you; feel the vital energy in your blood as it strengthens your magic; visualize yourself with lovers, men, women, friends, prosperity.

XIV. Relax and empty your mind, and masturbate (only if you are a man) while repeating:

Freya, bride of the Vanir.

Bring love to my heart.

Bring me the gifts of beauty.

Bring me the gifts of passion.

Bring me the gifts of wealth.

Oh, Freya, bring me the gifts of your nature.

Frey, bring me your power; grant me beauty, love, and pleasure.

Bring happiness, peace, and prosperity to my life.

XV. When you cum, say:

To Frey and Freya.

XVI. Mix the semen with saliva and offer to the gods saying:

Accept this fertile offering.

XVII. Relax again, focus on Frey and Freya, clear your mind, and meditate some time with them. When you finish, thank them and end the ritual.

I thank you, Freya, Mighty Goddess of Asgard.

Goddess of many names and virtues.

I thank you, Frey, Mighty God of Asgard.

God of many names and virtues.

May there always be peace between us.

I do not say goodbye but see you soon.

Hail Frey and Freya.

Note: if you are a woman, skip the masturbation part and go straight to the prayer and final thanks.

Aphrodite

You can see a description of Aphrodite in Chapter 3.

Things You Will Need

- Two red candles.
- A bottle of red wine.
- A wine glass (or water glass).
- Rose petals.

- A glass of water.
- A white bowl.
- Rose incense.
- A mirror bigger enough for you see your body, not necessarily the whole body at once but at least half of it.
- Ancient Greek music.

Step by Step

Purification

I. First, you need to purify yourself physically and spiritually. Take a bath to cleanse your body, and wear clean clothes. Meditate and clear your mind of all unholy thoughts. If it is possible for you and if you want to, you can go without eating meat for 24 hours before the ritual.

II. To purify the space, say:

Hekas hekas este bebeloi. Far, far from this place, be the profane.

III. Place your hand above the glass of water and say:

Creature of water, I consecrate you and awaken you immediately.

I purify the essence of this fluid so that it can expel and remove all negativity, and bless everything it touches.

IV. Sprinkle the space in which you are purifying with the consecrated water while saying:

I invite all harmful forces to leave right now. By the creature of water, may this place be blessed and I purified. I now proclaim the sacred silence.

V. Stay in silence for a moment visualizing the place being cleansed. Concentrate on a violet flame purifying and taking away all negative energy.

The ritual

I. In the center of the space in which you are working, put the bowl on the floor with a candle on each side. The incense should be behind it and all the other items in front of the bowl.

II. Burn the incense, light the candles, and call for Aphrodite seven times:

Aphrodite. Aphrodite. Aphrodite. Aphrodite. Aphrodite. Aphrodite. Aphrodite.

III. Continue:

Aphrodite, goddess of love, hear me.

Daughter of Zeus, goddess of pleasure, goddess of beauty, goddess of sexuality, I invoke you.

Goddess of beauty, share your secrets with me.

Show me how I can become beautiful to my eyes and everyone's eyes.

IV. Pour some wine into the wine glass, raise it, and say:

Accept this wine as my sacrifice. I give it to you with sincerity and love, but knowing you deserve more and more.

Send me your energy and shape my body the way I want it to be.

Goddess of beauty and love, make me the most beautiful human being that ever existed.

V. Raise the glass of water and say:

This is the elixir of life and beauty.

Without it, no man can survive, and no beauty lasts.

Then pour all the water into the bowl.

VI. Take the rose petals in your hands and say:

These are the perfect natural representation of beauty.

VII. Put the petals in the bowl and continue:

I now ask you, O Great Aphrodite, to send forth your energy into this bowl and turn this mixture into a divine liquid capable of healing all the imperfections of my body, including [say all the things you want to change in your body].

Now I offer you some music and dance.

VIII. Play ancient Greek music and dance around the bowl for some minutes.

IX. Take the bowl and say:

In the name of Aphrodite, I now change my body to the way I want it to be.

X. Spread the water over your whole body. Visualize all the imperfections fading away. Say out loud what is changing in you.

XI. Now take the mirror, look at you, and see how beautiful you are. Say it with conviction. Don't doubt it.

XII. Closing the temple

I thank you for your work on this day, Mighty and Beautiful Aphrodite. I now declare this temple closed.

CHAPTER 4

MONEY SPELLS

Money spells are where most people fail to achieve the desired effect. One can cast a spell to attract money every single month and still not get a single cent more than they already have. It happens because of the lack of objectivity; in other words, asking for money requires an existing source from where it will come. If you want to earn more money in your current job, so you must ask for a job promotion. If you want money by gambling, so ask for that and start betting.

The real problem when you don't specify the source where the money will come from is receiving the money in a very undesirable way. Imagine you suffering a car crash and getting compensation from your insurance, do you want that? I bet you don't. Besides, you should make it clear the spell must work without causing harm to anyone. You don't want to get promoted in your job because your coworker died. You should behave like this with every spell you cast, without harming yourself, your family, your friends, or anyone else.

Working with Bune

Bune, Bime, or Bim is a spirit that can bring money to those who call him. He is a powerful Duke who rules 30 legions of spirits.

Things You Will Need

- Two white candles.
- Incense (sandalwood).
- The seal of Bune.
- Well-made food prepared by yourself.

Step by Step

I. Perform the Banishing Ritual of the Pentagram.

II. Set up an altar with the Triangle of the Art, candles, offerings (food), and incense. Consecrate the triangle.

III. Write your intent on the back of the seal of Bune. For example, "I want to get promoted in my job." Put the seal inside the triangle.

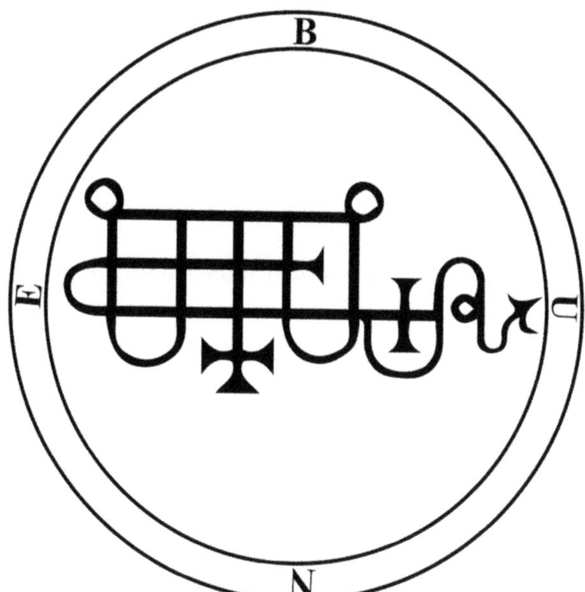

Figure 7. The seal of Bune

IV. Light the candles, burn the incense, and cast a circle.

V. Invoking Bune

Recite the following invocation three times:

Bune, Bime, Bim, Mighty and Powerful Duke, I invoke you.

In the name of the Most High, I call you, and I ask that you receive my requests.

Among the many gifts you possess, you master the art of wealth, bringing money to man, quickly and effectively.

Come and receive my sacrifice.

VI. Sacrifice and requests

I prepared this food especially for you, as a sign of respect for your great powers.

I ask your help with my financial problems.

I [insert your name] humbly request that you [insert your wish].

Grant my wish within [insert how many days you will give him to fulfill your requests] and without causing harm to myself, my family, my friends, or anyone else.

VII. Thanking Bune

I thank you, Great Duke Bune, for your presence in this rite.

You can now go back from where you came from, ready to fulfill what I have asked from you.

VIII. Close the circle and the triangle.

IX. Perform the Banishing Ritual of the Pentagram.

X. You can dispose of the food a few hours later.

XI. Keep the seal until your wish is fulfilled. Then you should deactivate it by saying:

This seal no longer represents a connection with the spirit Bune. You have no powers anymore.

Then burn it.

If the time you gave the spirit is over and your wish was not fulfilled, deactivate the seal and burn it. You can repeat the spell, but I advise that you try another one.

Working with Seere

Seere, Sear, or Seir is a mighty prince. He can bring money quickly to those who call him. He rules 26 legions of spirits, and he is often gentle when called. This prince doesn't require great sacrifices or offerings from the magician and will be happy with small things offered to him.

Things You Will Need

- Two white candles.
- Incense (cedar).
- Well-made food prepared by yourself.

Step by Step

I. Perform the Banishing Ritual of the Pentagram.

II. Set up an altar with the candles, offerings (food), and incense.

III. Burn the incense, light the candles, and cast a circle.

IV. Invoking Seere

Say the following sentence called ENN thirty times. ENNs are like phone numbers that link you directly to a spirit. Ideally, you should sing it, instead of just speaking it:

Jeden et Renich Seere tu tasa.

Then, say the following invocation 3x:

Seere, Sear, Seir, Mighty Prince, I invoke you.

Among the many gifts you possess, you can bring everything quickly, from anywhere in the world, and at any time.

Hear me and come to receive my sacrifice.

V. Sacrifice and requests

I prepared this food especially for you, as a sign of respect for your great powers.

I ask for your help with my financial problems.

I [insert your name] humbly request that you [insert your wish].

Grant my wish within [insert how many days you will give him to fulfill your requests] and without causing harm to myself, my family, my friends, or anyone else.

VI. Thanking Seere

I thank you, Prince Seere, for your presence in this rite.

You can now go back from where you came from, ready to fulfill what I have asked from you.

VII. Close the circle.

VIII. Perform the Banishing Ritual of the Pentagram.

IX. You can dispose of the food a few hours later.

Note: it is not the intention of this kind of spell to wait for any manifestation on the part of the spirit. Usually, this work is a one-way communication where only the magician/witch speaks. However, by pronouncing the ENN of Seere 30x as I instructed, Seere may manifest himself somehow, either through the incense smoke and candle flame, or even using the voice.

CHAPTER 5

MANIPULATION SPELL

This type of spell is useful when you want to change the mind and control someone's life or make someone take your side. You must already know this is a black magic spell; as previously explained, when you mess with somebody's life, you are doing nothing but black magic, and perhaps there are consequences for those who practice it.

Unlike the previous chapters where were presented two or more spells for each area, in chapter 6, I decided to include only one. This is because manipulation spells require a very powerful spirit that possesses the ability to manipulate people and will agree to do the job for you. When you work with spirits like Bune to get promoted in your job for example, he will have to manipulate your bosses, but this is different because you are not directly asking him to manipulate anyone. So, I can only think of a spirit that has the necessary requisites to perform this task, and he is Belial.

Working with Belial

Belial is a mighty king who governs 50 legions of spirits. He is believed to have been created right after Lucifer, so you can imagine how ancient and powerful he is. Working with Belial requires patience and confidence since he can completely ignore, manipulate, or deceive you if you think he is not great enough or if you show your weaknesses to him. A pre-ritual where you introduce yourself to Belial through prayers and offerings before calling him is the best way to get his collaboration.

Everyone who works with this spirit agrees on one point: he doesn't like being called a king. He occupies this position, but the best is always refer to him only as Belial.

Things You Will Need

- Three white candles.
- Incense (frankincense).
- Water, salt, food, objects, etc. Whatever you choose to offer him.
- The seal of Belial.
- Sterilized needle

Step by Step

Pre-ritual

I. Activating the seal of Belial

Hold the seal in your hand and gaze at it for three minutes. Absorb all the details in your mind. Then, say:

Seal, you now represent a connection with Belial. So mote it be.

Figure 8. The seal of Belial

II. Devotion

For three days before casting the spell, recite the following prayer to Belial and offer him a different thing each day:

> *Mighty and Powerful Belial, hear me. I come to you willing to receive your teachings and glory. Accept my sacrifice symbolized by this offering as a sign of our communion and respect.*

Keep silent for a moment. You can dispose of the offering a few hours later.

The ritual

I. Perform the Banishing Ritual of the Pentagram.

II. Set up the altar with the Triangle of the Art and incense. Put a candle on each edge of the triangle and consecrate it.

III. Put the seal inside the triangle, burn the incense, and light the candles.

IV. Cast a circle.

V. Invoke (3x):

O Mighty and Powerful Belial, great and feared, I invoke you.

I ask you to listen to me and be willing to receive my requests.

Your powers and abilities are what I need right now.

Wherever you are in the world, I invoke you, Belial.

VI. Sacrifice and requests

I humbly offer you this [insert the name of what you are offering] and a drop of my blood.

Listen to me and help me to [insert your wish].

Grant my wish within [insert how many days you will give him to fulfill your requests] and without causing harm to myself, my family, my friends, or anyone else.

Use a sterilized needle to pierce your finger and drip a drop of blood on the altar. This is necessary because you are asking Belial to manipulate someone, and this is not something easy to do. Your blood will provide more energy to Belial.

VII. Thanking the spirit

I thank you, spirit Belial for your help in this rite.

Your presence honors me because I know how powerful you are.

You can now go back from where you came from, ready to fulfill what I have asked from you.

VIII. Close the circle and the triangle.

IX. You can dispose of the offerings a few hours later.

X. Perform the Banishing Ritual of the Pentagram.

CHAPTER 6

FINDING ANSWERS

When we want to find answers for questions about the present or the future, we are talking about divination, which is a practice widely used by magicians and witches since it is considered a must-do before any magical operation. When we are preparing to perform an evocation or to cast a spell, we should try to find out what could possibly block our magic, if the entity we intend to call will help us, etc. The problem with divination is due to the complexity of its reliable methods like Tarot and scrying that requires dedication from the magician and at least months of practice.

Before writing this chapter when I was still wondering if I should include a discussion about divination in this book, I had a hard time deciding what reliable and accessible divination method I could teach in just a few pages. It would not be possible to explain how Tarot works because it would take half of a book. Scrying was also out of the question since you don't learn how to scry, that is a gift you are born with. Of course, you can practice scrying and try to develop this skill, but it will not be the same. The pendulum is another divination method that is considerably easy since you just need a small object hanging on a rope, but in my experience, pendulums are not suitable for divination. Most of the time, it gives you accurate answers only for things that your conscious or subconscious mind already knows. If you ask the pendulum questions about the future, you will probably get wrong answers since your subconscious doesn't know the answers yet. But pendulums can be useful if you are not sure about what directions you should take in your life because it can access your subconscious, which is a giant library that never forgets anything.

In this chapter, I present three divination methods that are easy to use and more efficient than a pendulum. First, you will learn how to discover the name of your guardian angel and demon. Once you know their names, you can ask them questions about your life because they know everything about you in the present and future time, and they have no reason to lie to you. The second method uses a simple pack of cards, and the last one is called free writing.

The Name of Your Guardian Angel and Demon

A guardian angel is an angel that follows you from the first day of your life until the last one. He guides and protects you in all phases of your life, even if you don't know he exists. A guardian demon acts in a similar manner but with less influence in your life since we tend to ignore and repel everything related to demons.

Demons are spirits that can't be called angels because, in a very distant time, they lost that status for some reason that we can't be sure about. But they are not spirits of hell as you may think. A magician must know that hell doesn't exist, and the astral plane is far more complicated than the simple Christian definition of heaven and hell.

Working with demons tends to be easier than working with angels. They come quickly and can better understand our mortal necessities while angels may have some difficulties. This not means you should avoid working with angels at all. They are really powerful creatures with many functions in the universe, and one of them is to help humans. They just need to trust you; in other words, you have to create a bond with them and not just ask for a one-time favor.

Method 1 – Pendulum

Although the pendulum is not a reliable way of divination, we are going to use it in the process of trying to find the name of your guardian angel or demon because I also provide here an easy way for you to check if the information you got from it is correct.

Calibrating the pendulum

If you are a beginner or if you are using a new pendulum, you need to calibrate it first.

I. Hold the pendulum between your thumb and index finger, always allowing it to swing freely. If you want, you can sit down and rest your elbow on a table in front of you.

II. Ask the pendulum "show me a yes," and it moves, showing you which movement means yes. Ask "show me a no" and see which movement means no.

III. Now ask obvious questions like "is my name [your name]?". Only stop asking obvious questions when you get only correct answers.

IV. Now that you have calibrated your pendulum, you need to make a bigger copy of the following table:

Table 2. Pendulum

1	2	3	4	5
6	7	8	9	A
B	C	D	E	F
G	H	I	J	K
L	M	N	O	P
Q	R	S	T	U
V	W	X	Y	Z

Preparation

I. Choose a quiet place to work.

II. Perform the Banishing Ritual of the Pentagram.

III. Take a pen and blank paper for you to write down the answers.

IV. Cast a circle.

V. Sit down inside the circle and relax for a while. Put the paper with the numbers and letters on the ground in front of you.

VI. Give your pendulum the following instructions:

Pendulum, you are going to move only over the right numbers and letters.

Asking the pendulum

I. Hold the pendulum and start asking the following questions:

1. *How many letters have the name of my guardian angel/demon?* – Place the pendulum over each number for 5-10 seconds. When it moves, you got your answer.
2. *What is the first letter of my guardian angel's/demon's name?* – Place the pendulum over each letter till you get the right one. Repeat it for the following letters according to the number you got in the first question.

II. After finishing with the questions, close the circle and perform the Banishing Ritual of the Pentagram.

Checking the information

I. Go to google.com and search for angel/demon + name, example: demon Aym; angel Haniel.

II. If you find any result related to angels or demons, what you got from the pendulum is correct.

III. In case you could not find anything useful on Google, repeat the search using quotes. Example: "demon Aym"; "angel Haniel."

If even after using quotes, you don't get any results related to angels or demons, it means that either the name of your guardian spirit isn't on the internet or the pendulum didn't work for you. In this case, you have one last option you could try.

IV. Search for names of angels and demons, and study their pattern. Generally, these names share some similarities. Compare them with the names you have. If they have nothing in common, forget it and try using the Ouija Board, our next subject.

Method 2 - Ouija Board

The Ouija Board, also known as Spirit Board, is a tool used to contact spirits in order to get answers from them. This is also not a recommended method for divination because there is a high probability that when using it, you are, in fact, talking to yourself, or the spirits are lying to you. Another negative point is that we don't know what kind of spirits we are dealing with.

When using the board, a door is automatically open, and any kind of spirit can come through to talk to the practitioner. This is why you should use the board always with someone else to prevent you from being too vulnerable to be deceived by the spirits. Another reason you should not use it alone is to prevent your mind from interfering in the answers. So, follow all the recommendations given below.

Figure 9. Ouija Board

Note: only use the board if the pendulum didn't work for you. Don't use it to check if the information the pendulum gave you is correct.

Using the board

I. Perform the Banishing Ritual of the Pentagram.

II. Cast a circle wide enough for two people.

III. These two people that we are going to call "operators" must sit down inside the circle with the board in front of them.

IV. The operators place their index fingers on the planchette. Don't put much pressure on it.

V. One of the operators ask:

Are there any spirits here willing to answer my questions?

VI. When you get a yes, proceed to the following question:

Have you ever lived?

VII. If the answer is yes, go to the section Closing the Board. This is because only spirits of dead people would answer yes to this question, and they have nothing to offer you.

VIII. If the answer is no, ask the next question:

What is your name?

IX. If the spirit refuses to give you his name, say:

I am the ruler of this place. Those who want to participate in this ritual must say their names because this is my rule. Say your name right now or leave.

X. If the spirit refuses to give his name again, go to the section Closing the Board and try again later. Otherwise, you can continue with the next question.

XI. Show your authority to the spirit:

I am the governor of this place, and I have established a major rule. You must give only true answers to all my questions. Are you willing to follow this rule?

XII. If the answer is no, close the board, if it is yes, proceed:

What is the name of my guardian angel/demon?

XIII. Write down the name given. Don't ask any more questions. Don't be tempted to ask questions about your personal life.

Closing the board

I. Once you got the name of your angel or demon, you must close the door you opened. Start it by saying:

> *I thank you for answering my questions, and now I say goodbye.*

II. Wait for the planchette to move towards the "goodbye" on the table. Whatever if it moves or not, you must say the following:

> *All my questions were answered, and now all the entities present here must leave. In the name of ADONAI, and in my name, the ruler of this place, I declare this temple closed.*

III. Turn the board upside down.

IV. Close the circle and perform the Banishing Ritual of the Pentagram.

Checking the information

Repeat the same process to verify the information received, used in the pendulum section. If you don't get positive results, I am afraid the board also didn't work for you. Of course, it is possible that the names of your guardian spirits are not on the internet, or their names have nothing in common with the names of other angels and demons, but it is not a good sign.

Establishing Contact

Once you have the name of your angel or your demon, it is time to contact him. You should work only with one of them at least until you get more experience and decide for yourself it is safe to have two different spirits guiding you.

Make a prayer with your own words, saying you truly want him to reveal himself to you. Recite it every day until you feel his presence more and more. Before the prayer, you should vibrate the name of your guardian angel or demon for about two minutes. You may also try to find his seal on the internet; it would be very helpful. If you find the seal, use it before the prayer, gazing at it while you vibrate his name. Clear your mind and meditate, waiting for any sign from him. He can contact you through almost any means, including dreams, the internet, movies, etc. You could be watching a movie, and suddenly some character says something that grabs your attention and immediately makes you think about your guardian angel or demon; this is a message from him.

Once the contact has been established, you can use a pendulum to ask questions, as long as you feel their presence first because using a pendulum without making sure your angel/demon is with you, will not give you good results. Other ways to receive answers will depend on the bond between you and them. They will show what will work best for you.

Getting Answers from a Deck of Cards

The cards have powers and can give us answers to almost everything in our lives, showing us the future or, more commonly, the paths we should follow. The Tarot and Gypsy Deck are the two most used methods of divination through cards. The Tarot is more complex and has more than seventy different cards with each card representing a different meaning. Both the Tarot and Gypsy Deck are not suitable for yes or no questions. They can't specifically answer if your boyfriend is cheating on you or if you will marry someday. If you ask them something like this, the chances of you getting even more confused are high. That is why many Tarot readers will not allow their clients to ask specific questions.

A simple deck of cards can be transformed into a magical tool for divination, ideal for everyday questions. You can use it to ask if you should go to a party, if you should call someone, or even if you should or not cast a spell. Unfortunately, like all the other yes or no oracles, questions about the future can't be properly answered. So, avoid asking what you will happen in your life.

Step by Step

I. Buy a new deck of playing cards.

II. Write YES on the Nine of Hearts and NO on the Nine of Spades.

III. Usually, a deck comes with two Jokers, but you are going to use only one, the other you put aside. The Joker is the MAYBE card.

Consecrating the deck

The deck must be consecrated to the four elements; otherwise, it will have no powers.

I. You will need incense (any type), a glass of water, a candle, and salt or soil.

II. Go to the place where you consecrate your tools and set up an altar in a space where you can walk around it. Put the deck on the altar.

III. In the area around the altar put the incense in the east, the candle in the south, the glass of water in the west, and the salt in the north.

IV. Go to the west of the altar, face east and open the temple saying:

I call the highest forces in the universe to guide me in this ritual. The intention of this work is to consecrate and give the necessary powers for this deck of cards to become a magical tool capable of answering everything I ask it.

V. Go to the east, burn the incense, and say:

I invoke the guardians of the east, powerful sylphs. Lend me the powers of the air, so I can do what I must do today.

VI. Go to the south, light the candle, and say:

I invoke the guardians of the south, powerful salamanders. Lend me the powers of fire so I can do what I must do today.

VII. Go to the west, take the glass of water, and say:

I invoke the guardians of the west, powerful undines. Lend me the powers of water so I can do what I must do today.

VIII. Go to the north and take some salt in your hands. Say:

I invoke the guardians of the north, powerful gnomes. Lend me the powers of the earth, so I can do what I must do today.

IX. Take the deck, go to the east, and say:

May the guardians of the east consecrate and empower this deck of cards.

Pass the deck through the incense smoke.

Repeat the same action in the south, west, and north. Important: you don't pass the deck through the candle flame. Holding the candle in one hand and the deck in the other while asking the guardians of the south to consecrate it is enough. The same goes for water. Water can damage it, so be careful.

X. After finishing in the north, spread the cards over the altar. Point your wand at the deck and say:

Deck of cards, you are now magical. By the powers of the air, fire, water, and earth, you are now able to answer any questions correctly. The Nine of Hearts means yes; the Nine of Spades means no, and the Joker means maybe. To answer my questions, you must go through all dimensions of the universe, past, future, and return with accurate answers. So mote it be.

XI. Go to each direction, starting by east, and say:

I thank the guardians of the [insert direction] for your help today. I now close the portal of the [insert direction].

XII. Go to the west of the altar, face east, and say:

I thank the highest forces in the universe for allowing this work to happen. I now declare this temple closed.

Using the deck

I. Sit down in a comfortable position and concentrate on what you want to know. Ask your question out loud, addressing the deck.

II. Shuffle the cards the best you can — the more shuffled, the better. While shuffling, ask the question again.

III. Put the deck in front of you like the following image.

Figure 10. Playing card

IV. Cut the deck two times from left to right.

Figure 11. Cutting the deck

V. Put the deck back together again, placing the piles on top of each other from left to right.

VI. Now start turning over the cards one by one in a left to right movement until you reach a yes, a no, or a maybe. For example, if you reach the yes first, this is your answer.

Don't ask the same question again. If you do this, you will probably get a different answer, and this will mess with your mind. You have to accept the first answer as the right one. This is how divination works. You can choose another method of shuffling and cutting the cards. It is up to you in case you have a better one.

Free Writing

There is a method of divination called automatic writing that is similar to my free writing one but with a difference. To use the automatic writing, you take a pen or pencil, a sheet of paper, sit at a table, relax, and start writing what comes to your mind. This can work, and you should try it if you want. The method I am going to teach here is different because instead of you writing what comes to your mind, your hand automatic moves the pen, and you don't control when it starts and when it stops. I consider that this technique was developed by myself because this idea came to my mind without seeing anything similar anywhere before.

Step by Step

I. If you wish, you can invoke some god that you believe in, or any other entity that you think can give you answers. Take a pen and sheet of paper. Sit down at a table or anywhere you can write comfortably.

II. Relax your body and mind. Forget about the rest of the world.

III. Put the sheet on the table and position the pen over it without putting much pressure.

IV. Give instructions on how you want to receive the answers. For example, say:

> *All the questions I ask here must be answered with a Y meaning yes and an N meaning no.*

V. Close your eyes and ask your question aloud.

Your hand will start moving in less than a minute. Don't put much pressure on the pen.

VI. After you finished, open your eyes and see if you got a Y or an N. This is your answer.

CHAPTER 7

SELF-PROTECTION

No matter if you occasionally cast a spell or if you are an active witch or magician, you need to protect yourself. Threats can come from anywhere, including someone close to you or entities that you work with. Generally, If you follow the basic rules to work with spirits, they will not cause you any harm, and the worst they can do is to refuse to work with you. When it comes to people, you can't control their actions; you can't prevent someone from cursing you or putting a black magic spell on you. But what you can and must do is to prepare your aura to be able to block these unwanted energies. When you are ready for something, you will not be taken by surprise.

In this chapter, we are going to learn the best protection techniques against the dangers of the occult world. If you follow the tips given here, you can be sure that nothing bad sent through the spiritual world will reach you.

Balancing Your Energy

Have you ever found yourself in a situation where you were off-balance? For example, when you are standing on the bus, you need to hold onto the handrails to prevent you from falling over or when you are drunk and can't properly walk. These are concrete examples, but the principle is the same with our aura. When your energy field is operating only in one direction, receiving or losing, it is off-balance. The same happens when your energy field is weak since it is not getting the energy it needs to keep things going right in your life. These changes are so significant that an advanced psychic can notice there is something wrong with your aura only by looking at you.

The consequences of an off-balance energy are many, and your life can turn into a complete mess. You can get sick, lose your job, go through hard times in your relationship, get depressed, etc. Most people don't even notice that maybe something is wrong with them because they are used to it since this is a process that tends to occur gradually. So, they see it as a bad phase instead of fixing the source of the problem.

Banishing and Invoking

In some parts of this book, you are instructed to perform the Banishing Ritual of the Pentagram before and/or after a ritual. When used before any magical work, it is useful to tune the magician with the highest forces in the universe, bringing the Tree of Life into the aura. Crowley, in one of his books, shared some information about this exercise. The following quote explains exactly what I just said:

> *"The habitual use of the Lesser Banishing Ritual of the Pentagram (say, thrice daily) for months and years and constant assumption of the God-form of*

Harpocrates (See Equinox, I, II and Liber 333, cap. XXV for both of these) should make the "real circle", i.e. the aura of the magus, impregnable.

This aura should be clean-cut, resilient, radiant, iridescent, brilliant, glittering. "A soap-bubble of razor-steel, streaming with light from within" is my first attempt at description; and is not bad, despite its incongruities."

The BRP also can cleanse one's energetic environment of chaotic energies. The problem starts when you use it on a daily basis without any kind of invocation. You are banishing things from your life and not receiving any. So, to avoid this, you need to invoke first and banish twelve or more hours later, or banish first and invoke right away.

Suggested practice

In the morning: invoke the four elements. Instructions on how to do this can be found in the Appendix.
At night: banish the four elements (see the Appendix).

Perform this exercise three times a week if everything is going well in your life, and you want to keep it that way, or daily if you feel things could be a lot better or if nothing is working for you.

Building a Shield Around You

When working with magic, one of the first things you learn is you must develop a strong visualization technique. A variety of exercises and rituals demand the magician to really see what they are doing. When you draw a pentagram in the air, you must see it there; even if you turn around, you know there is a pentagram right behind you. This is necessary because our mind has the power to manifest things in the physical and astral world. Of course, it is a lot more complicated to do on the physical plane because we have something called the Laws of Physics, but on the astral level, it is quite easier since there are no limitations there. In this exercise, we are going to use our mind to create a shield around our aura, working with some key colors.

Colored cards

Prepare some paper cards in gold, dark red, and violet. Alternatively, you can use images on your smartphone, tablet, or computer instead of paper.

Gold: this color will attract divine protection to you.

Dark red: you will be a stronger person, always ready to face any difficult situation.

Violet: this color must be visualized in flames. It will cleanse your aura of all negativity at all existing levels.

Step by step

I. Use each color on a different day. My suggested order is violet, gold, and dark red.

II. Choose a quiet place where you can deeply relax. Sit in a comfortable position.

III. Hold the target color in front of your eyes. Stare at it for five minutes. Then put the paper card or device aside, relax your body, and close your eyes.

IV. Visualize yourself in the center of an empty place. This place is in the color you are working with. The color in the form of abstract light begins to emerge from all directions coming directly to your body. This colored light is now surrounding your whole body.

V. Imagine as if you were charging your batteries with this light. Feel the energy flowing through you.

VI. Keep doing this exercise for ten minutes. Then you can open your eyes, and it is done.

Don't forget that when working with the violet color, you must visualize it as flames and not as light.

Amulets

Amulets are objects of protection with names and symbols engraved on it, representing the forces in which the object is connected, offering protection to those who use it. One of the most famous amulets are the seals of Solomon, also called pentacles. I sometimes use the Fourth Pentacle of the Moon to protect me against evil sorceries.

I restored all the three pentacles presented here to provide them with a better quality since the manuscripts where they are from are more than 500 years old.

Instructions for All Planetary Amulets

I. Drawing, copying, and consecration must be done in the hour of the planet.

II. Ideally, you should draw the amulet on a blank sheet of paper using the color of the planet, but you can make a copy of it using a xerox machine as well.

III. All amulets must be consecrated to the four elements before you can use them.

The Third Pentacle of Jupiter

This will defend and protect you against all kinds of spirits, especially the ones you evoke.

Figure 12. The Third Pentacle of Jupiter

The Sixth Pentacle of Jupiter

This protects against all earthly dangers.

Figure 13. The Sixth Pentacle of Jupiter

The Fourth Pentacle of the Moon

This protects against all evil sorceries and from all injury to soul and body.

Figure 14. The Fourth Pentacle of the Moon

Activating the Pentacles of Solomon

All three pentacles presented in this chapter must be activated each time you use them. You do this by holding the pentacle in one hand while reading the corresponding Bible verse.

The Third Pentacle of Jupiter: Psalm 125: 1.

The Sixth Pentacle of Jupiter: Psalm 22:16-17.

The Fourth Pentacle of the Moon: Jeremiah 17:18.

APPENDIX

Invoking and Banishing the Four Elements

The Qabalistic Cross

All the spheres of light in this ritual are formed from the same source of light. Other versions of it ask us to imagine those spheres without mentioning where their energy is coming from. I consider it a mistake, and that is why I created a modified version of the Qabalistic Cross.

I. Go to the east and face east. Stand with feet together and arms close to the body. Imagine that a sphere of brilliant white light is descending far from above your head. This sphere is about 10 inches or 25 centimeters in diameter, and now it is right just above your head.

II. With a dagger, wand, or your right index finger, touch the light and bring a fraction of it to the forehead. This smaller sphere is half the size of the one above your head. Touch the forehead and vibrate ATAH.

III. Touch the light again, but this time, point towards your feet and imagine the sphere of light descending to the ground. Vibrate MALKUTH.

IV. Now bring another sphere of light to the right shoulder. Touch the shoulder and vibrate VE-GEBURAH.

V. Bring another sphere to the left shoulder. Touch the shoulder and vibrate VE-GEDULAH.

VI. Put your hands together in front of your chest and vibrate LE-OLAHM. Now clearly imagine the four spheres of light forming a cross and this cross entering your body, filling it with pure light.

VII. Still with hands together vibrate AMEN.

Drawing the Pentagrams

Here you choose if you want to banish or invoke the four elements. The only difference is in the pentagrams you need to draw in this step. The following image gives you both the banishing and invoking versions.

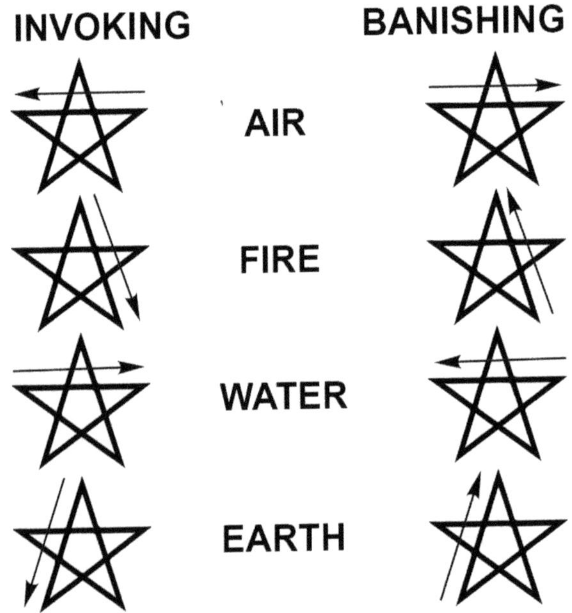

Figure 15. Invoking and banishing pentagrams

I. In the east, facing east, draw in the air the appropriate Pentagram of Air and then bring the point of your finger to its center. Vibrate the name YHVH.

II. Without moving your finger in any other direction, start tracing a circle while you move to the south. In the south, trace the appropriate Pentagram of Fire. Bring your finger to the center and vibrate ADNI.

III. Continue the semi-circle to the west and trace the Pentagram of Water, bringing your finger to its center. Vibrate AHIH.

IV. Repeat the same process to the north with the Pentagram of Earth. Vibrate the name AGLA ATAH GIBOR LE-OLAHM.

V. Now complete the circle bringing your finger to the center of the pentagram you drew in the east.

VI. Now in the east, stay in cross position (feet together and arms extended) and say:

Before me, the great Archangel RAPHAEL (vibrate).

Behind me, the great Archangel GABRIEL (vibrate).

At my right hand, the great Archangel MICHAEL (vibrate).

At my left hand, the great Archangel AURIEL (vibrate).

VII. Now say:

About me, flame the pentagrams.

Imagine the circle and the pentagrams in white flames.

And in the column shines the six-rayed star.

Imagine two hexagrams, one under and one above you, shining and forming a grid of light around your body.

VIII. Repeat the Qabalistic Cross, and the ritual is done.

Developing Your Sensitive Abilities

These techniques will work better if you already have the necessary abilities, but they are not fully developed. On the contrary, you can achieve some level of sensitivity, but you will have to work harder on a daily basis.

Exercise 1

I. Go to the internet and download any Shamanic meditation music. Transfer it to your smartphone or any other device where you can plug earphones.

II. Take three equal coins and mark them with any hydrographic pen. For example, write A, B, C. You can also use playing cards of different suits, credit cards, etc. The purpose here is to use objects with the same dimensions but with something different in each one of them.

III. Go to a quiet place and put three cushions in front of where you will sit.

IV. Take the three objects in your hands, close your eyes, and mix them. Still with eyes closed, put each object under a different cushion.

V. Sit down in a comfortable position, put on the earphones, and play Shamanic music.

VI. Close your eyes and relax. Think about one of the objects in front of you. Go through your mind under each one of the cushions and try to locate it. Take your time.

VII. When you are ready, open your eyes and check if you are right.

Practice this exercise daily until you guess right where the three objects are. Then you can start working with more objects until you are ready to locate them without the help of Shamanic music.

Exercise 2

This exercise is called the Middle Pillar Ritual, and it helps to build the Tree of Life within the aura.

I. Perform the Qabalistic Cross.

II. Stand facing west, feet together, arms close to the body, and palms facing forward. On your right is the Black Pillar of Severity. On your left is the White Pillar of Mercy. You are in the middle representing the Pillar of Balance.

III. An incredibly bright white light, the Light of the Infinite-Self, originates far above your head.

IV. The light descends to the top of your forehead (Kether), forming a sphere the size of your head. Strongly vibrate the name: AHIH (pronounced "eh-heh-yeh").

V. Now imagine a shaft of light descending from your forehead to the throat region (Daath) and forming another sphere of light. Strongly vibrate the name: YHVH ALHIM ("ye-hoh-vah el-oh-heem").

VI. Now a shaft of light descends from your throat to the chest (Tiphareth), forming a new sphere of light. Strongly vibrate the name: YHVH ALOAH ve-DAATH ("ye-ho-vah el-oh-ah veh da-ath").

VII. Visualize a shaft of light descending from your chest to your genital region (Yesod) and forming a sphere of light. Strongly vibrate the name: SHADDAI AL CHAI ("shah-die el hai").

VIII. Finally, a shaft of light descends from your genital region to your feet (Malkuth), forming a new sphere of light that touches the floor. Strongly vibrate the name: ADNI HARTZ ("ah-doh-nye ha-rets").

IX. Now visualize the sphere at your feet rising and absorbing the light and energy of all the other spheres until it reaches your head. Now only one sphere exists. Imagine it circulating through your body from left to right. Keep doing it for three minutes, at least.

www.ingramcontent.com/pod-product-compliance
Ingram Content Group UK Ltd.
Pitfield, Milton Keynes, MK11 3LW, UK
UKHW021924190726
13853UKWH00002B/832

9 788799 982943